THE GF KID
A CELIAC DISEASE SURVIVAL GUIDE

WRITTEN BY
MELISSA LONDON

ILLUSTRATED BY
ERIC GLICKMAN

Woodbine House 2005

All rights reserved. Published in the United States of America by
Woodbine House, Inc., 6510 Bells Mill Road, Bethesda, MD 20817. 800-843-7323. www.woodbinehouse.com

Library of Congress Cataloging-in-Publication Data

London, Melissa.
   The GF kid : a celiac disease survival guide / written by Melissa London ; illustrated by Eric Glickman.— 1st ed.
      p. cm.
   ISBN-13: 978-1-890627-69-0 (pbk.)
   ISBN-10: 1-890627-69-0 (pbk.)
  1. Celiac disease. 2. Celiac disease—Diet therapy.   I. Glickman, Eric. II. Title.
   RC862.C44L66 2005
   616.3'99—dc22

                                                                    2005013226

Manufactured in China

First Edition

10   9   8   7   6   5   4   3   2   1

To Paris,
for making it look so darn easy to be a GF kid.

And to Jolie & Trey,
for being the best siblings a GF kid could ever have.

We love you guys.

Mom & Dad

Thanks to Ann Whelan,

*editor and publisher of **Gluten-Free Living Magazine**,*

for all your help and knowledge.

Hi, my name is Paris.
I'm 11 years old. And I have celiac disease.

It's pronounced
Silly-ACK

"Thank you, Thank you." I have 1 brother and 1 sister and 2 fish. I wish I had a dog, but my Mom is allergic! AHH-CHOO!! Bless you. Thank you, You're welcome. Don't mention it! I'm in 6th grade and I love writing...(DUH!) And acting. My friends call me the Drama Queen. (APPLAUSE!!!)

That means I can't eat regular bread, cake, cookies, pasta, or pizza.

Ever again.

... OR regular donuts, cupcakes, muffins, biscuits, crackers, croutons, granola bars, bagels, pretzels, pastries, pies, rolls, matzo, ice cream cones, breadcrumbs, cereal, macaroni, lasagna, noodles, stuffing, gravy, etc, etc, etc. UGH!!!

"Why?" you must be wondering.
What's wrong with those foods?

Well, they all have gluten.
Gluten is in wheat, rye, oats, barley, and malt.

Gluten is in all baked goods and lots of other stuff too.
It's kind of like the "glue"
that holds some kinds of food together.

My body thinks that gluten is a poison.

When I eat, let's say, a bagel, the gluten goes through my body.
When it gets to my small intestines, my antibodies
come to fight the "poison."
That's what antibodies do to protect us.

This is a dramatization.
I wouldn't really
eat a bagel anymore!

But since there really isn't a poison there,
the antibodies end up hurting my small intestines.
When that happens, I can't get the nutrients from the food I eat.
No matter how much I eat.

There are lots of things that can go wrong with you when this happens.

Some kids have lots of bellyaches.

Some kids have to go to the bathroom. A lot.

Some kids get really crabby.

Some kids are tired. All the time.

Before I was diagnosed with celiac disease I was the same size as my sister and she is 3 years younger than me! Sometimes people thought we were twins!! E-M-B-A-R-R-A-S-S-I-N-G!!!

Some kids are very short. (That's what happened to me.)

And some kids seem to have nothing wrong at all.
But their bodies are still being hurt inside.

The good news is:
All I have to do to get better is stop eating gluten.

The bad news is:
That is **really** hard.

When I go to a party,
I can't have the pizza or the cake.

When I go to a restaurant,
I can't have chicken nuggets or grilled cheese.

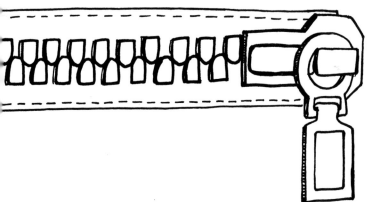

used to it and it became _much_ easier. I don't let C.D. ever stop me from doin

I was totally freaked out and angry when I was first diagnosed. But after a while, I got

Sometimes it makes me sad.

anything with my family or friends that I used to do. It's just food! Some kids have way, way, _way_ bigger problems!!! Sometimes I just need to remind myself of that!

Now I can only eat foods that are gluten free.

POTATOES

EGGS

PLAIN CHICKEN

PICKLES

CHEDDAR CHEESE

JELL-O

MANGOS

MILK

PEAS

PLAIN STEAK

WHIPPED CREAM

PLAIN YOGURT

In my house we call that GF.

WATERMELON　　**BUTTER**　　**PLAIN RICE**

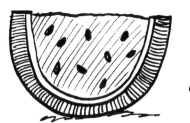

PLAIN PORK CHOPS　**PEANUT BUTTER**　**SORBET**

BANANAS　　**CORN ON THE COB**　　**PLAIN NUTS**

SODA　　**STRAWBERRIES**　　**TUNA**

There's **lots** of food I can eat at the regular supermarket.
And we go to the health food store for
GF bread, cereal, cookies, pretzels, pizza, and pasta.
Sometimes we order stuff online.

HERE ARE SOME COMPANIES I GET GF FOOD FROM

Amy's Kitchen
www.amys.com   (707) 578-7188

Chebe bread
www.chebe.com   (800) 217-9510

Dietary Specialties
www.dietspec.com   (888) 640-2800

EnviroKidz Organic
www.envirokidz.com   (604) 248-8777

Food for Life Baking Co.
www.food-for-life.com   (800) 797-5090

Foods by George
www.foodsbygeorge.com   (201) 612-9700

The Gluten-Free Pantry
www.glutenfree.com   (800) 291-8386

Glutino
www.glutino.com   (800) 363-3438

Happy Happy Happy
www.happyhappyhappy.com   (212) 254-4088

Kinnikinnick Foods
www.kinnikinnick.com   (877) 503-4466

Mr. Ritts Bakery
www.mrritts.com   (877) MRRITTS

Shabtai Gourmet
www.shabtaigourmet.com   (516) 374-7976

The Really Great Food Company
www.reallygreatfoods.com   (800) 593-5377

Van's International Foods
www.vansintl.com   (310) 320-8611

This is what I take to school for lunch now.

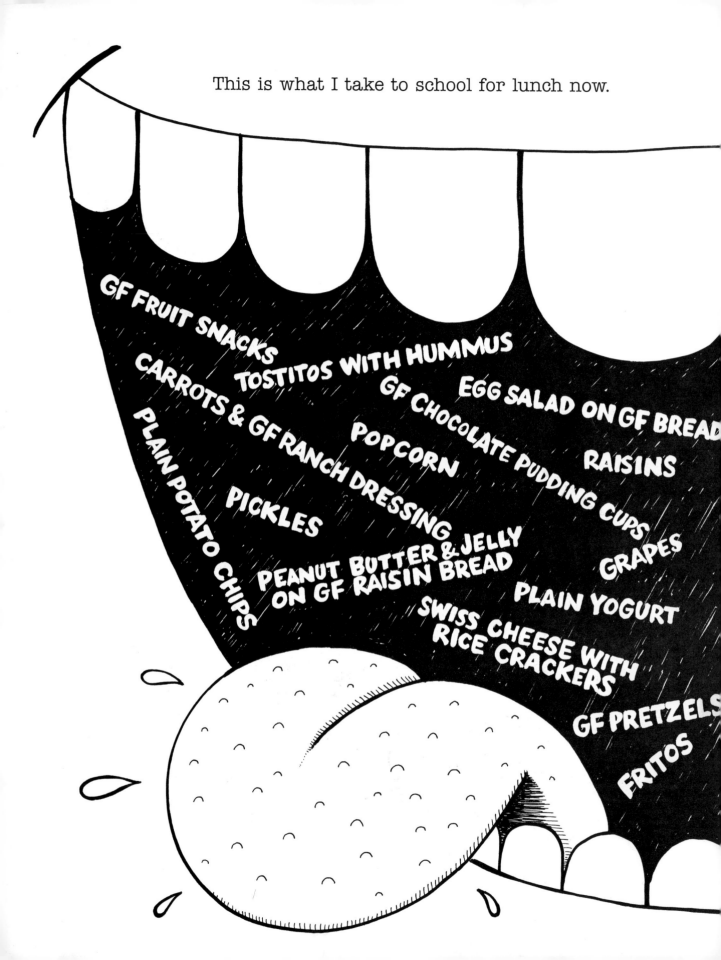

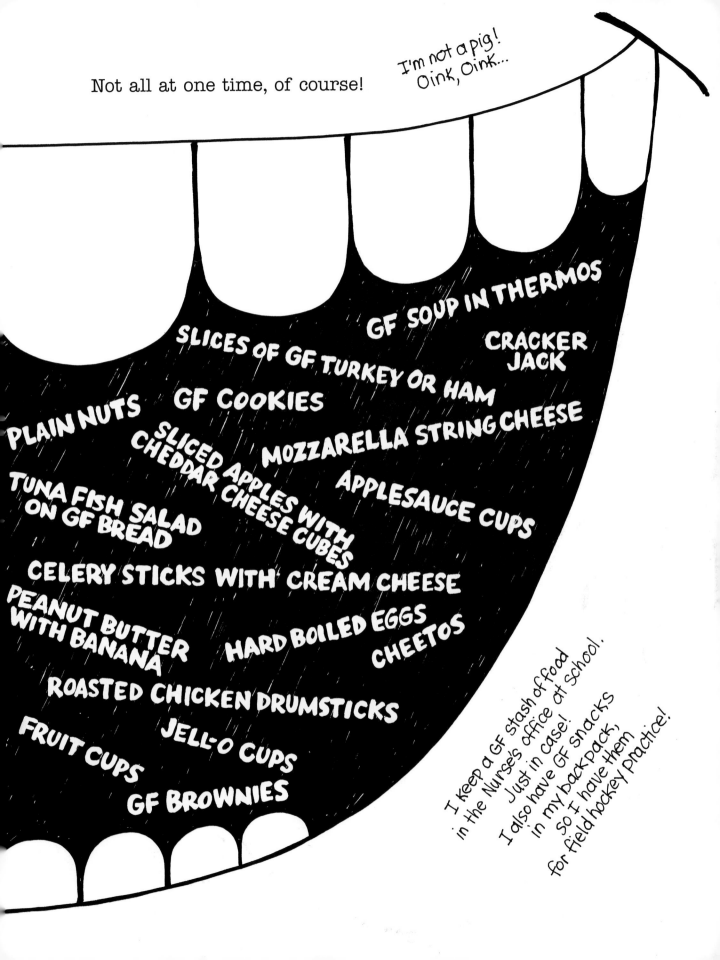

When I first found out I had celiac disease,
I was so worried about how my friends would react.
I didn't want them to think I was weird, with my "special" diet.

But my friends are amazing.
Believe it or not, they actually find the whole thing kind of interesting!

When it comes to telling other people, what I say all depends
on how well I know them . . . and my mood.

(Sometimes it does get annoying.)

When I go to a party now, I usually have to bring my own food and dessert.
At first I wasn't too thrilled about this.
But now it's a piece of cake. (A GF one, of course!)

I love the smell the candle makes after you blow it out & make a wish!

At **my** birthday this year, we had make-your-own sundaes instead of cake. My friends were psyched!

Happy Birthday to Me!

Instead of ordering pizza at my party, my Dad BBQ'd burgers & GF hot dogs (everyone else had regular buns).

My mom was **totally** neurotic
the first time I went on a sleepover.
She was so worried I was going to get "glutenfied"
that she packed me enough GF food to last a month!

It wasn't such a big deal.
I had a GF pizza for dinner and we had eggs for breakfast.

My mom has calmed down since then.
(A little, anyway.)

I made that word up!

Speaking of pizza, you never realize
how much pizza people eat until you have celiac disease.

When my friends go out for pizza now, I always go.
Either I bring something I can eat
or I **try** to find something GF on the menu.
My parents told me they'd rather me have a bag of chips and a soda
than miss out on the fun. That's OK with me!

Going to the movies is just as fun as it used to be.
I can have plain popcorn, soda, and candy. I **love** the movies!

NOW PLAYING

CD ALSO STANDS FOR "CAN DO"

STUFF I CAN EAT

Starring
PLAIN POPCORN · JUNIOR MINTS
SNO-CAPS · RAISINETS · SODA POP

GF | GLUTEN-FREE
Appropriate for kids with CD

I like to sit 3/4 of the way down in the movies.
Not 2 close, Not 2 far, Just right!

But NO Twizzlers...they have flour in them. Who knew?

The best news of all is that tons of candy is GF.
Halloween isn't hard at all! And if I get any "gluteny" candy,
I just trade with my sister and brother for a piece I can eat.

I made up
that word too!

My sister was a Devil
this year. How appropriate!
Just kidding!!!

♥ My favorite GF candy ♥

Hershey's milk chocolate bar
Reese's Pieces
3 Musketeers
Tootsie Rolls
Tootsie Roll Pops
Hershey's Kisses
Reese's Peanut Butter Cups
M & M's (plain & peanut)
Baby Ruth
Butterfinger
Skittles
Starburst
Charms Blow Pop
Goobers
Raisinets
Snickers
SweeTarts
Wonka Bottle Caps
Wonka Nerds
Wonka Laffy Taffy
Spree
Trident Gum

GLUTENY CANDY
CAN'T EAT EVER!

Cookie Dough Bites
Nestle Crunch
Kit Kat
Twix
Twizzlers
Whoppers
Buncha Crunch

Trick or Treat
smell my feet...
Give me something
GF to eat!

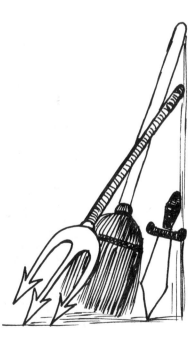

When you have celiac disease you have to
read the labels on the foods you eat to make sure they're safe.
(Gluten is hidden in many foods that you would never suspect!)

At first, my Mom did this for me. But now I know how to read labels.
If I'm not sure if something is GF or not,
I'll call the company and ask them myself.
There is usually a 1-800 number right on the package!

I interrupt this book for a brief but important message.
You know that little star thing that means you need to read the tiny type
at the bottom of the page? Well, here is one.

★ Even if I list a food as GF in this book, you still have to read the ingredients and call the company yourself, because ingredients change all the time! Thank you. You can go back to the book now. Go! Get outta here!

Here are some safe ingredients.

Amaranth
Annatto
Arrowroot
Ascorbic Acid
Aspartame
Balsamic Vinegar
Beta Carotene
Buckwheat
Calcium Carbonate
Canola Oil
Carob Bean
Carob Flour
Carrageenan
Citric Acid
Corn Flour
Corn Meal
Cornstarch
Corn Syrup
Cream of Tartar
Dextrose
Distilled Vinegar
Flax
Fructose
Gelatin
Grits, Corn
Guar Gum
Herbs
Honey
Hydrolyzed Soy Protein

Xcellent!

Perfect!

2 cool!

Yeah!

Way to go!

1derful!

Gr8!

Awesome!

You Rock!

Super!

What is this?

Job's Tears
Kasha (roasted buckwheat)
Lactic Acid
Lactose
Lentil
Locust Bean Gum
Malic Acid
Maltitol
Maltodextrin (in food made in USA)
Millet
MSG (made in USA)
Polenta
Potato Flour
Quinoa
Rennet
Rice Flour
Sodium Citrate
Sodium Nitrate
Sorghum
Soy
Soy Lecithin
Sucrose
Tapioca Flour
Vanilla
Vanillin
Whey
Wines
Xanthan Gum

Go there to print out the complete lists!

Reprinted by permission of www.celiac.com

Here are some **FORBIDDEN** ingredients.

Read this with an eerie, scary voice!

Barley	Semolina Triticum
Barley Malt	Small Spelt
Beer	Soy Sauce
Bleached Flour	Spelt (Triticum Spelta)
Bran	Spirits (specific types)
Brewer's Yeast	Tabbouleh
Brown Flour	Teriyaki Sauce
Bulgur Wheat/Nuts	Textured Vegetable Protein
Couscous	Triticale
Durum Wheat	Udon (wheat noodles)
Farina Graham	Wheat
Filler	Wheat Bran Extract
Flour	Wheat Durum Triticum
Graham Flour	Wheat Germ Oil
Hydrolyzed Wheat Gluten	Wheat Nuts
Hydrolyzed Wheat Protein	Wheat Starch
Hydrolyzed Wheat Starch	
Kamut	
Malt	

BOO!

NO!

The following may or may not be GF. Check with manufacturer.

Malt Extract	Artificial Color
Malt Flavoring	Caramel Color
Malt Syrup	Dextrins
Malt Vinegar	Flavoring
Matzo Semolina	Gravy Cubes
Oats	Miso
Pasta	Modified Food Starch
Pearl Barley	Mono and Diglycerides
Rice Malt	Stock Cubes
Rye	
Semolina	

HISS!

2 bad!

You stink!

No way!

Curse you!

LOSER!

Gluten is in soooooo many things, it is unbelievable!
Some of the places are really weird.

USUALLY NOT GF

USUALLY NOT GF

USUALLY NOT GF

NOT GF
(Even when I'm 21!)

NOT GF
(I can't have most california rolls.)

MAY NOT BE GF

MAY NOT BE GF

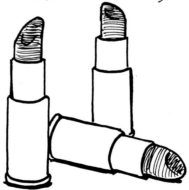

MAY NOT BE GF
(Boys don't have to worry about this.)

NOT GF
(I gotta wash my hands after playing)

And I can never assume anything.
Just because it is not in one thing doesn't mean it's not in another.
I **always** have to read the labels.

I have to be careful about something else too.
Contamination.
I have to make sure my GF food doesn't get "gluteny" by accident.

Not in 2023 I can't eat french fries if they are fried in the same oil as breaded stuff, like chicken nuggets or onion rings.

P.S.
McDonald's fries are GF! YES!!!

I don't really have a suit like this!

I can't put my GF bread in a toaster filled with regular crumbs. We have 2 toasters now.
1- 4 me.
1- 4 everyone else.

I need my own jar of peanut butter, jelly, cream cheese, and butter, so gluteny crumbs don't get in from people making sandwiches, etc.

BUTTER

I need my own colander too. Regular pasta leaves gooey stuff in all those little holes. (Did you ever count the holes in your colander? Mine has 290!)

I can't eat a hamburger once it's been on a bun. I need my burger to be put right on the plate!

A few months ago I accidentally ate some gluten.
It was at my cousin's wedding and I tasted an appetizer
that **seemed** like it would be ok.

Oh my god, I had the worst stomachache and headache ever.
I ended up missing most of the party!

Actual Size
↓

This is the culprit!
It was some
bacon, vegetable, cheese
thing in a sauce.
(It wasn't even good. Ugh!)

Remind me,
when I get married,
not to have these
at the wedding!!!

When you have celiac disease, there are two rules you have to live by.

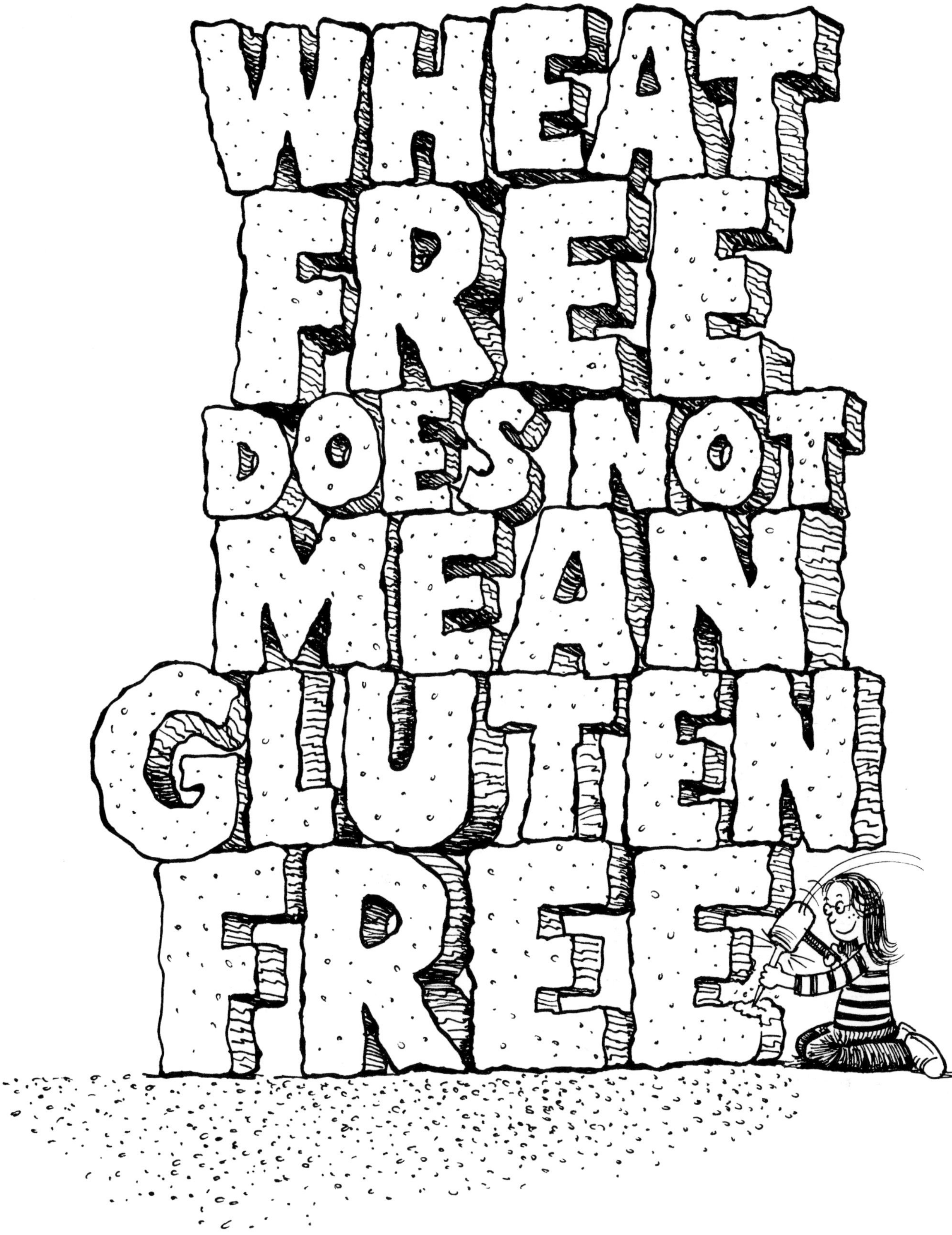
WHEAT
FREE
DOES NOT
MEAN
GLUTEN
FREE

I still go to restaurants, although it's pretty tricky now.
When I order I don't explain the whole celiac disease thing.
I usually just tell them that I'm "allergic" to wheat.
That they get!

NOT true!

P.F. Chang's China Bistro & Outback Steakhouse have special GF menus that you can ask for! Put a shrimp on the barbie for me, Mate!

Fast food restaurants are the easiest place to eat, as long as you do your homework before you go. Some have GF menus online, like mcdonalds.com & wendys.com Hit print- and go!

It definitely takes **a lot** of extra planning to go on a vacation when you have celiac disease. But it is totally worth it.

We went to Disney World last year and it was amazing.
You can prearrange GF meals at some of the restaurants there!
They made me GF spaghetti, GF chicken nuggets,
GF rolls, and GF cookies!
Now is that "a dream come true" or what?

We pack an extra box or suitcase filled with GF goodies. Like cereal, pretzels, cookies, etc.

We pre-ordered a GF meal for the plane. It was pretty gross... but trust me, it wasn't worse than anyone else's!

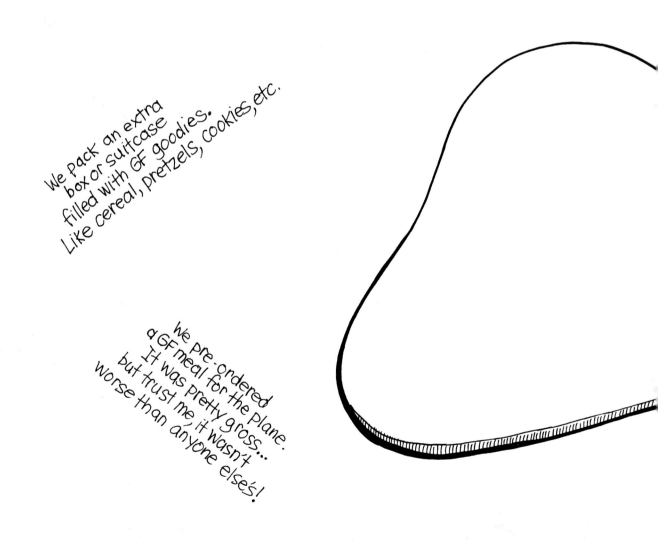

I once read somewhere that some scientists think the reason
so many people can't eat gluten is because
we were never intended to.
If you think about it, the cavemen (and women)
weren't exactly dining on spaghetti and garlic bread!

Celiac disease was discovered in Holland during World War II.
There were a whole bunch of kids who were always sick.
Because of the war, there was a wheat shortage
and "miraculously" the sick children got better.
Isn't that cool? I love that story!

← I've always wanted shoes like these!

You may not know anyone else with celiac disease now. But you will. It is not uncommon, and more and more kids (and grown-ups) are being diagnosed with it every day.

Approximately 1 in every 133 people has celiac disease. That's like millions of people!!

My neighbors Isabel and Lily have it.

A new boy at school has it.

A friend at sleep-away camp has it, too.

Don't get me wrong...
I'm not a giant or anything—
but at least now
my little sister
looks like my _little_ sister!!!

I've grown a lot since I stopped eating gluten.
And my insides are healthy now, too.

I'm no different than any other kid.
I'm just a GF kid!

The End!

Turn for some more good GF Stuff!

Here are some of my favorite GF recipes.

YUM ♥

Potato Chip Fried Chicken

- Chicken (with bone or without)
- 12 oz. bag Lay's Classic Potato Chips crushed into tiny pieces
- 2 eggs (whipped)
- Oil (olive or canola)

Dip chicken in egg mixture and then roll in potato chip pieces until well coated. Fry in pan in oil until brown or bake in oven until thoroughly cooked inside. My friends <u>love</u> it!!!

Sandwich Minis

- Tostitos Restaurant Style Tortilla Chips
- GF tuna salad, turkey, cheese, egg salad, hummus, or whatever!

Take one Tostitos and put whatever you like for lunch on it. (I love egg salad or hummus.) Cover with another Tostitos. Voila! You've got lunch! Crunch, crunch, crunch, crunch, crunch. Now make more.

Marshmallow Treats

- 3 Tbsp. butter or GF margarine
- 6 cups Erewhon Crispy Brown Rice GF Cereal
- 10 oz. Kraft Jet-Puffed Marshmallows
- PAM Original Cooking Spray

Melt butter in large saucepan over low heat. Add marshmallows and stir until completely melted. Remove from heat. Add cereal and mix until well coated. Using spatula (sprayed with PAM) press into 9x13 pan (sprayed with PAM). Cut into squares when cool.

Try 1 you'll want S'more! HA! HA!

Banana S'mores

- Bananas
- Kraft Jet-Puffed Mini Marshmallows
- Nestle Semi-Sweet Chocolate Morsels
- Aluminum foil
- Campfire, fireplace, or grill

Peel open 1 side and cut slit lengthwise in banana. Stick marshmallows & chocolate chips into slit. Close peel back up and wrap tightly in foil. Put in campfire and cook for 5 minutes until melted. Take out and cool. Open and eat with a spoon or just stick your face in it! Yum!

They are really easy to make and taste great. Try them!

Waffle Egg Sandwich

- 2 GF waffles
- 2 eggs scrambled
- 1 tablespoon butter
- 1 slice real cheese (optional)

Scramble eggs in pan with butter and melt cheese on top if you want. Toast waffles. Put eggs on 1 waffle and top with the other. This is a great breakfast. Time for school!

EGGcellent!

Chocolate Fruit Breakfast

- 4 GF mini waffles
- Nutella Hazelnut Spread
- Sliced strawberries, bananas, and blueberries

Toast the waffles and spread Nutella on top. Then top each with some fruit. You're done! I'm obsessed with Nutella! You got to try it. You can make this with peanut butter too!

You'll have a BALL making these!

Grilled Cheese Quesadilla

- 1 corn tortilla
- ½ cup shredded cheddar cheese
- 1 tablespoon butter
- Chopped tomatoes, sliced olives, and sour cream (optional)

Melt butter in pan and then put tortilla in. Sprinkle cheese on top and let melt. Put tomatoes and olives on if you want. Then fold in half and put on plate. You can make this in the microwave too! Adios!

Chocolate Covered Peanut Butter Balls

- 1 cup plain peanut butter
- 1 cup powdered sugar
- 1 cup chopped nuts (I use almonds)
- 2 tablespoons melted butter
- 1 teaspoon vanilla
- 24 oz. Nestle Semi-Sweet Chocolate Morsels

Mix everything (except chips) in a bowl. Make little balls and put on wax paper. Melt chocolate (I use the microwave). Using toothpicks, dip balls in chocolate and put on wax paper. Put in refrigerator to harden.

Hey, if you want to learn more, check these out.

Celiac Disease Center at
Columbia University
161 Fort Washington Ave., Suite 645
New York, NY 10032
(212) 342-0251
www.celiacdiseasecenter.columbia.edu

Celiac Disease Foundation
13251 Ventura Blvd., #1
Studio City, CA 91604
(818) 990-2354
www.celiac.org

Celiac Sprue Association
(Cel-Kids Network)
P.O. Box 31700
Omaha, NE 68131-0700
(877) CSA-4-CSA - Toll free
www.csaceliacs.org

Gluten Intolerance Group (GIG)
15110 10th Ave. SW, Suite A
Seattle, WA 98166
(206) 246-6652
www.gluten.net

National Foundation
for Celiac Awareness
124 South Maple St.
Ambler, PA 19002
info@celiacawareness.org
www.celiacawareness.org

University of Maryland
School of Medicine
Center for Celiac Research
20 Penn St., Room S303B
Baltimore, MD 21201
(410) 706-8021
www.celiaccenter.org

"HERE I COME TO SAVE THE DAY!
THE GF KID IS ON THE WAY!"

GF

GO TERPS!

Here's where you can get all kinds of GF food.

The Gluten-Free Mall
www.glutenfreemall.com

Gluten Solutions, Inc.
www.glutensolutions.com
(888) 845-8836

The Dietary Shoppe
www.dietaryshoppe.com
(215) 242-5302

Whole Foods Market
www.wholefoods.com
There are stores all
over the place.

YUM!

BURP!

These are really good support groups.

ROX MY SOX!

R.O.C.K. Raising our Celiac Kids
(Groups throughout the country)
(858) 395-5421
ROCK@celiackids.com
www.celiackids.com

Westchester Celiac Sprue
Support Group—Celiac Kids Club
(Meets in Westchester, NY)
info@westchesterceliacs.org
www.westchesterceliacs.org

HI! WE HAVE CELIAC, TOO!

How about some books & magazines?

Gluten-Free Living Magazine
19A Broadway
Hawthorne, NY 10532
(914) 741-5420
www.glutenfreeliving.com

**Incredible Edible Gluten-Free
Foods for Kids:
150 Family-Tested Recipes**
By Sheri L. Sanderson
Published by Woodbine House
www.woodbinehouse.com

**Kids with Celiac Disease:
A Family Guide to Raising Happy,
Healthy, Gluten-Free Children**
(Your <u>parents</u> definitely need this one!)
By Danna Korn
Published by Woodbine House

**Wheat-Free, Gluten-Free Cookbook
for Kids and Busy Adults**
By Connie Sarros
Published by McGraw-Hill

These are cool websites.

**Bob & Ruth's Gluten-Free
Dining & Travel Club**
www.bobandruths.com

Celiac.com
www.celiac.com
info@celiac.com

Celiac Chicks
www.celiacchicks.com

Celiac Teens
www.celiacteens.com

TWEET!
TWEET! TWEET!*

*WE HAVE CELIAC, TOO!

Celiac Listserv at St. Johns University
(A listserv is kind of like a group e-mailing list
where you can ask questions and people will
answer from around the world.) To join send
an e-mail message to: LISTSERV@MAELSTROM.
STJOHNS.EDU write, "subscribe celiac" with
your first and last name in the body of the
message.

**Gluten-Free Restaurant
Awareness Program**
www.glutenfreerestaurants.org
info@glutenfreerestaurants.org

COMPUTER
MOUSE

Looking for a summer camp? These are totally GF!

**Camp Celiac—Sponsored by
Celiac Sprue Association**
Ages 7-16
csgc@ix.netcom.com
celiacs@csaceliacs.org
(877)CSA-4CSA
www.csaceliacs.org/CampCeliac.php

**GIG Kids Camp—Sponsored by
Gluten Intolerance Group**
Ages 7-18
info@gluten.net
(206)246-6652
www.gluten.net

Did you know that this is a **true** story?

Well, it is. Except for the fact that I don't wear the same striped shirt every single day.

I was always a healthy, happy, and active kid. I never had bellyaches or diarrhea. I was just really, really small.

At my 10-year-old check-up, the doctor said that I wasn't growing like I should be. So I had to go see a Pediatric Endocrinologist (a doctor who specializes in hormones and growing and stuff like that).

For a <u>year</u> I was poked, pinched, and prodded. I even had to run in the doctor's office with my winter coat on, so that I would sweat, to test my growth hormone level! They found nothing wrong. That doctor (I will not mention his name) wanted to give me growth hormone anyway. (A shot every day for 2 years! Yikes!)

Well, luckily my parents took me to another doctor for a second opinion. (I will mention his name, Dr. Robert Rapaport.) He saw me once, took blood, and called 5 days later saying that I tested positive for celiac disease! I had an endoscopy at the hospital(it wasn't too horrible), and they said I 100% had celiac disease. My intestines were so badly damaged that the doctors could not believe I never had stomachaches or anything like that!

From that point on, I went totally GF. Within one year I gained fifteen pounds and grew almost five inches! One of my friends at camp, who was also really small, then tested positive too. Her parents had taken her to doctors for years, but no one ever tested her for celiac disease. Not too many doctors in this country know enough about it.

After I was diagnosed, my mom read everything there was about celiac disease. But there was nothing for me to read. And I <u>love</u> to read. That year in school, we had to do a nonfiction report on something. I did it on celiac disease. (It was 22 pages long and I got an A+.) That gave my mom the idea to write a children's book, to help other kids like me. My dad did the illustrations.

I hope you like the book. And I hope it makes it a <u>little</u> easier to be a GF kid!

TTYL!